CONTENT PAGE

1. Chapter 1 - Introduction
2. Chapter 2 - Debunking Myths
3. Chapter 3 - Buy and Hold Strategy
4. Chapter 4 – Price earnings ratio and its importance to the Investor
5. Chapter 5 - Risk management
6. Chapter 6 - Get over your emotional attachments to money
7. Chapter 7- Invest in something you know a lot and care about
8. Chapter 8 - 10 Quick to-do list as a professional Investor

Book

Introduction

This book is designed to enlighten and guide you in your journey in mastering stock trading and enable both new and existing investors to attain higher winning percentage rather than loss percentage. One of the best ways to invest money is to purchase assets that either create income, increase in value, or do both. Some assets may only appreciate in price, such as gold, diamond or silver, etc. You buy them with the idea that they'll be worth more in the future so you can sell them for a profit. And some assets may only give you income, such as a bond that pays a fixed amount of interest.

Investments that offer the potential for both income and price appreciation include:

- Rental property
- Businesses
- Stocks

This e-book will focus on stock trading

CHAPTER ONE

INTRODUCTION TO STOCK TRADING

In a world driven by advancement in technology and Knowledge, in the last decade, we have experienced a very quick growth in companies and corporations; this has given birth to new industries while some existing industries went into extinction.

In this fast-moving world, a fast train which has been in the world for many years has re-emerged as one of the vehicles of wealth and profit maximization.

In recent times, Stock trading has been in trend for a while. Come to think of it, is it profitable to all investors that are into stock trading?

According to Chandra Shekhar, he observed that around 85 to 90% of people lose money in stock markets or are stuck in some form of bad investment due to wrong entry. However, only 10% to 15% of successful people invest & trade wisely to earn handsome profits from stock markets. Having heard this, it will be of importance to master stock trading before deciding to take it as an opportunity or an occupation.

Basics of the stock market

The main reason why individuals would love to invest their cash in the stock market is for everyone to generate money through the stock market. Either through the use of a phone (i.e. via phone calls) or using the internet from a computer.

Stocks allows you to own successful companies, this among many other reasons is why they are good investments, and they have been the best investment over time. The equity of a company can be owned from the comfort of your home, so stocks are also known as equities. Investing in stocks can aid both the investor and the company. You are entitled to own an establishment on the basis of the stock you have acquired.

Becoming a Stockholder is a good idea, this is because the wealth of a company is maximized when a company prospers, and so does the owner of the company. Its wealth is also maximized, so as the owner of the company. Companies want you to buy its stocks because it wants to use your money to develop better products, get new equipment, and broaden its activities.

Trading is the process of purchasing a stock and reselling the same stock. However, trading is quite easy to do, it can be done quickly either by making a phone call or with the internet by clicking the mouse. Before the advancement of technology, trading activities were usually carried out through the use of paper, but now, the world is fully computerized.

You can make money by owning stocks is through the capital appreciation strategies such as buy and hold and dividends stock. The establishment pays the dividend every quarter year. Money is being generated through capital appreciation by purchasing at a cheaper rate and selling it at a high rate. The overall profit, in this case, is the money generated from the capital appreciation of the stocks.

Stock represents a claim on the company's assets and earnings. As you acquire more stock, your ownership stake in the company becomes greater."

Types of Investors in the stock market

Bulls: Investors who make money from rising stock prices are called Bullish investors.

Bears: Investors who buy stocks that are crashing or falling in prices, Bearish investors.

Sheep: Investors, who lose money, follow the herd, get slaughtered by the market.

The goal of every investor is to make more earnings from trading stock, but I advise that your goal should not only make earnings but also the concept of positive expectancy must be mastered by the investor, this supported Nick Radge.

Chapter 2

Debunking the myths

Warren Buffet once said that he would never try to make money on the stock market. Rather, he buys with the assumption that the market could be closed the next day.

Investing in stocks can be said to be profiting, but it has not been the same story for everyone involved in stocks, as many investors wonder whether or not investing in stocks is worth all the trouble. Concurrently, however, it's very vital to maintain a realistic view of the stock market. Without considering the apparent difficulty, the regular myth about the stock market often arise.

Here are some of those myths

1. Gambling And Investing In Stocks Are The Same.

This belief among many others influences a lot of individuals to ignorantly leave the stock market. A lot of proficiency is required on the part of the stock trader while trading in the stock market. This implies that he or she must understand the dynamics in the trading environment. This is why many people shy away from the stock market.

When an investor buys stocks (common stocks), he owns a fraction of the company. The holder is authorized to make a claim on the assets and also a fraction of the profits that the company generates after their financial year. Frequently, shares are being considered as a trading vehicle, and they forget that stock represents the ownership of a company.

Investors are persistently trying to assess the profit that will be left over for shareholders in the stock market. This is why stock prices fluctuate. The outlook for business conditions is always dynamic, and so are the future earnings of a company.

It is not quite easy to assess the worth of a company. There are so many factors that cause the short-term price movements to appear to be random (academics call this the Random Walk Theory); however, over the long term, a company is supposed to be worth the present value of the profits it will make. A company can survive in the near future without profits because of the expectations of future earnings, but no company can fool investors forever—eventually, a company's stock price can be expected to show the true value of the firm.

Gambling is a win or loss game. It takes money from a loser and gives it to a winner. No value is ever created. The aggregate of an economy's wealth is increased through investing. As companies compete, they enhance productivity and develop products that can make our lives better. Don't flummox the creation of wealth and making investments with the gambling win or loss game.

2. Do not time the market

There is no particular time to trade in or trade out. What you must understand as an investor in the stock market is "consistency."

The investor's ability to minimize risk when stock trading result in a downturn, makes one a successful investor in the stock market. While there are numerous sophisticated strategies of managing threat within a portfolio, even the use of a moving average crossover, such as a fundamental method of price analysis, can be a valuable tool over long-term keeping periods.

The chart below indicates a simple moving average crossover study. In clarity, a simple form of price movement analysis can supply a beneficial identification of periods when portfolio risk are reduced, although the actual moving averages used are not importan

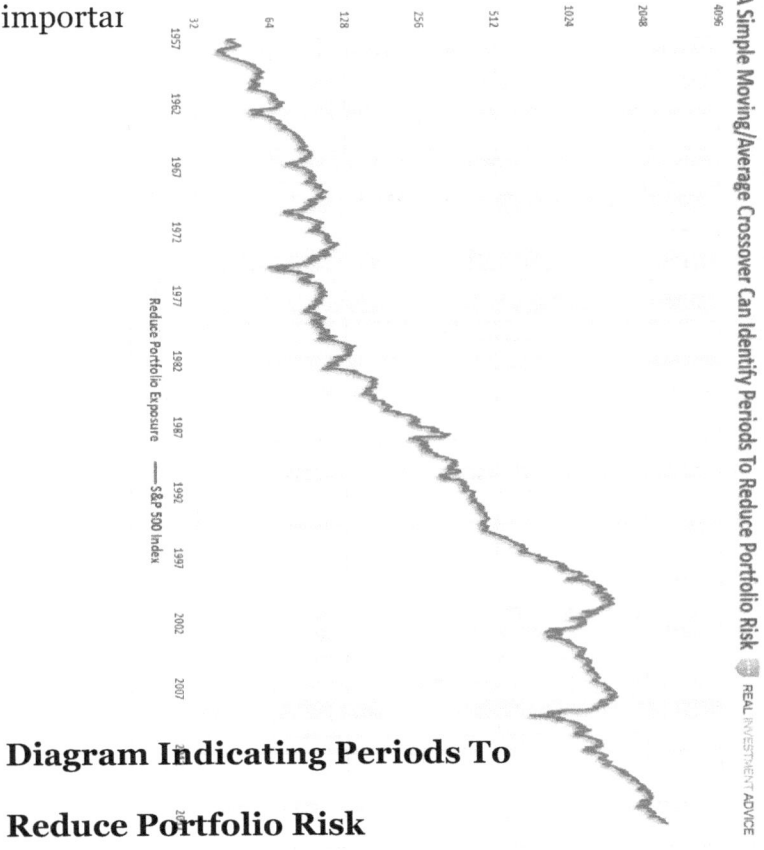

Diagram Indicating Periods To Reduce Portfolio Risk

Again, I am not pronouncing that such signals mean going one hundred percent to cash. I am implying that it is time for some basic portfolio risk management when sell indicators are given.

If any strategy is being used, whether basic or technical evaluation to reduce portfolio risk as prices/valuations rise, the long-term outcomes of fending off periods of extreme capital loss will outweigh missed short-term gains. Small changes can have a considerable impact in the long run.

3. "Buy and hold" and "dollar cost average."

While these two mantras have been the core of Wall Street's annuitization and commoditization of the investing business through turning unstable fee revenue into an easy circulate of income, they have really not labored for investors who were sold the "scheme." Two of the major reasons for the underperformances have been the destruction of investor capital and investor psychology.

Despite the analogy behind buying and maintaining stocks over the long term, the biggest single setback to the success over time is psychology. The behavioral bias that leads to poor funding decision-making is the total contributor to underperformance over time. Dalbar defined nine of the irrational investment conduct biases, but the two largest are the herding impact and loss aversion.

Herding effect is seen as behavior that represents the tendency of an investor(s) to mimic the actions of a larger group, whether those actions are rational or irrational. In many cases, herd behavior is a set of decisions and actions that an individual would not necessarily make on his or her own. The disadvantage of this behavior is that other investors trading environment is not exactly like yours, so there is much tendency that their investment decision will not work for you.

Loss aversion is an irrational investment behavior biases that occur when investors focus obsessively on one investment that's losing money, even if the rest of their portfolio is in the black. It has an adverse effect on investors trading decision. For example the pain of letting go a lost stock at the expense of their portfolio.

Those two behaviors tend to work side by side, compounding investor mistakes over time. Ever since the continual increase in the establishment of markets individuals are led to believe that the current price trend will continue for an indefinite period. As the financial markets evolve into a euphoric state, the beliefs become more established as the rising trends increases, until the last of holdouts finally buys in, as the financial markets evolve into a euphoric state.

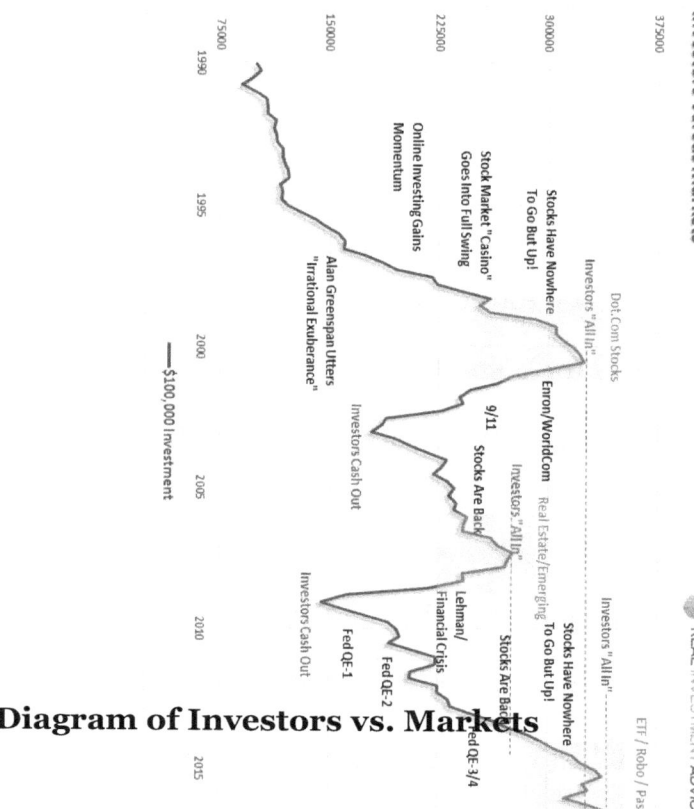

Diagram of Investors vs. Markets

As the markets reduce, investors gradually realize they are looking at something greater than a "buy the dip" opportunity. As losses mount, anxiety pushes buyers to attempt to keep away from additional losses that occur when you sell.

This trend in stock trading behavior seems counter-intuitive to the "buy low/sell high" investment rule and consistently leads to poor investment returns over time.

4. More risk equals more return

Investors are usually triggered to take on extra exposure to equities to improve the potential for higher charges of return if everything goes right. But every now and then, the deal does not constantly go as planned . "risk," is is "to expose something of value to risk or loss."

Michael Lebowitz his study cited that:

For many of the great investors, the main problem is no longer the attainable return but the chance and size of a loss.

Werner Heisenberg has an adaptation of the Hays Office where he believes that no matter how many times he looks into the future using an imaginary horoscope, the future would always be changing. To him, the future is in a state of constant flux.

Werner Heisenberg's adaptation of the Hays Office—the so-called principle of uncertainty whereby the act of measuring something has the effect of altering the measurement—is of such importance. Hence, you cannot actually see into the future. The most advisable thing to do is to analyze historical trends and make investment decisions based on that.

In planning to build up your wealth, wasting your investment time frame on your previous loss with the aim of making up for your mistakes is not an ideal strategy.

6. Cash is for losers

To a lot of individuals, holding cash is unwise, this mentality had been passed to lots of investors many times. To them, you are not only declining yourself of series of opportunities on the rocketing bull market but also your money is being eroded by "inflation."

Taking your money and investing it into the second-most-overvalued market in history is the main problem.

The advantages of having the capital to invest at lower valuations, while cash lost its relative purchasing power due to inflation resulted in an outperformance compared with waiting for previously destroyed investment capital to recover.

A lot of the mainstream media will quickly disagree with the concept of holding cash and tout long-term returns as the reason to remain invested in both good times and bad. The challenge here is that your money is at risk and most individuals' lack the time necessary to truly capture 30- to 60-year return averages.

7. If you're not in, you're missing out

Periods when there are low returns are always succeeded by times when the market has excessive valuations. Hence, you should realize that your timing of investment goes a long way in determining how much you eventually make.

8. Fallen Angels Will Rise Again, Eventually.

I am not sure who started this myth or the reason a lot of investors think this to be true. However, it is very harmful for you to think that a stock that has traded for 52 weeks or even more without making any profits is a good buy. It's just like the common Wall Street adage which says foolishness is when you try to catch a falling knife. There is no faster way to get hurt.

Let's look at two stocks for example:

- X got to an all-time high of $200 in the previous year but has dropped since to $40 per share.
- Y is a company of a small size which has just increased from $20 to $40 per share.

Which stock would you buy? Believe it or not, all other factors remaining constant, most investors will choose the fallen stocks. This is because they are convinced that such a stock will still achieve winning ways. If you are among this crop of investors in your thought pattern, you are committing investment suicide.

Price is just a single part of the investing equation (or, in other words, trading, which utilizes specialized investigation). The objective is to purchase great organizations at a sensible price. Purchasing organizations exclusively in light of the fact that their market price has fallen will accomplish nothing for you. Ensure you don't mistake this training for value investing, or, in other words, quality organizations that are undervalued by the market.

9. Stocks that go up must come down.

The law of gravity is not applicable to the stock market. There's no force of gravity which will pull down rising stocks. More than 20 years back, Berkshire Hathaway's stock price went from $7,455 to $17,250 per share in somewhat more than a multi-year time span. Had you felt that this stock would come back to its lower starting position, you would have passed up the ensuing ascent to over $303,000 per share toward the start of 2018.

We're not attempting to disclose to you that stocks never experience an amendment. The fact of the matter is that the stock price is an impression of the organization. On the off chance that you locate an incredible firm kept running by great directors, there is no reason the stock won't continue going up.

Stock price goes up only in exceptional cases.

10. A Little Knowledge Is Better Than None

Availability of historical, present and red-hot information i.e. will guide the investor accurately during his prediction of stock price movement in the short term and long term. Knowing something is generally better than nothing, but it is crucial in the stock market that individual investors have an in-depth understanding of what they are doing with their money. Investors who do their homework (detailed forecast of the stock market) are the ones that succeed.

On the off chance that you don't have room schedule-wise to completely comprehend what to do with your cash, at that point having a counsel is definitely not a terrible thing. You can choose to be a passive investor while your advisor does the monitoring of your stock. The expense of investing in something that you don't completely comprehend far exceeds the expense of utilizing an investment advisor.

Highlights:

- No one can depend on these myths if they want to succeed financially.

- Again, if the above-mentioned myths were true, a lot of people will retire as rich people.

- Eventually, only three things matter in long-term investing:

➢ How much you invest

➢ The time you sell

➢ The amount of risk you are willing to take

If you make any error in the three, you will achieve less success than you should have in stock investing.

If everyone believed the myths of life, the Airplane and telephone would only be Dreams.

Chapter 3

Buy and hold strategy

One of the funny things you see in the stock market is that every time one person buys, another sells, while both think they are astute.

    -**William Feather**

Meaning of Buy and Hold

There are several investment strategies used by investors in the stock market. The most widespread and widely accepted strategy is the buy and hold. This strategy is used mostly by investors interested in long-term investment. The buy and hold strategy requires patience and proper timing.

Buy and hold also known as positioning strategy is an investment strategy where an investor buys stocks in one or several firms and holds them for a long-term with the expectation that stocks will gradually increase in value over a long period of time. In a buy and hold strategy, investors can gain in two major ways, high rate of return or "cash out" (sale of shares when the value is highest).

The stock market is characterized by a high degree of volatility. This is why many investors tend to bail out at after a decline in the short run not knowing that the long run financial markets give a good rate of return. For example, a good buy and hold strategy would be the purchase of Apple stock in January 2008. During this period, if an investor had bought 100 shares at its closing price of $18 per share and held onto the stock until July 2016, when the stock was then worth $104 per share. That means that you are gaining a return of more than 500% in just eight years.

Forms of Buy and Hold Strategy

Investors under the buy and hold strategy can be grouped into; passive investors and active investors. In a **passive buy and hold investing**, an investor buys a portion of all the stocks that mirror returns of benchmark indexes such as; the Dow Jones Industrial Average (DJIA) or the S&P 500. A passive investor has no interest in short-term price movements and technical indicators. They make use of passive elements, such as dollar-cost averaging and index funds, while focusing more on building a portfolio than on security research and selection.

The mediocre returns achieved through the use of passive buy and hold investing has made some investors opt for an **active buy and hold investing strategy.** Active buy and hold involve purchasing stock predicted by portfolio managers to appreciate in value over time. This strategy attempts to secure certainty of high returns in the long run and thus eliminating the risk of holding on to stocks that will never increase in value. However, the risk that the investor's predictions being wrong can never be eliminated. In fact, research has shown that most active buy and hold investors lack the ability to generate returns in excess of a benchmark index and that most even fail to match the returns of major indexes. We can conclude and say that it is safer to stick with a passive buy and hold investing strategy, especially for first-time investors. However, what does not work for most people may favor some.

Highlights:

Tips to Enhance the Success of the Buy and Hold Strategy

- A factor that can improve the performance of Buy and Hold is the regular reinvestment of dividend. Instead of treating your dividend as a source of cash flow for settling one-off expenses such as trips or home improvement. Dividends can be reinvested to generate an even greater return in the long run.

- One crucial aspect of buy-and-hold trading is the eventual sale of the security. Buy-and-hold traders have to know when it's time to exit a position, even if they planned to hold onto the stock for the very long term. A good time to sell off your stock may be when a company files for bankruptcy or when the company goes through a major adjustment of strategy, it may also be time to reevaluate a holding.

Chapter 4

Price-earnings ratio and its importance to the Investor

Everyone has the brainpower to follow the stock market. If you made it through fifth-grade math, you can do it.

Peter Lynch

Stock price

As an investor, knowing what stock price is, is not enough. but understanding the stock price movements is what differentiate you from starters. The stock price is simply the amount of money it will cost to purchase a share of a company or fund. Stock prices can vacillate dependent on various variables. In the event that an organization discharges a gleaming income report, at that point financial specialists will probably feel more optimistic about its potential profitability. Demand for the stock will climb, thus will its price. Then again, if an organization reports negative profit or is the subject of bad press, its stock price can quickly fall.

P/E ratio

The P/E ratio is a way you can measure the relationship between a company's stock price and its earnings per share of stock issued. The P/E ratio is calculated by dividing a company's current stock price by its earnings per share (EPS). If you don't know the EPS, you can calculate it by subtracting a company's preferred dividends paid from its net income, and then dividing the result by the number of shares outstanding.

Let's say a company has a net income of $1 billion, it pays $200 million in preferred dividends, and it has 400 million shares outstanding. Here's how we'd calculate its EPS:

($1 billion - $200 million) / 400 million shares = $2 per share

Now that we know the EPS, we can figure out the P/E ratio. If the stock is currently trading at $30 per share, then the P/E ratio would simply be $30 divided by $2, or 15.

Stock price and P/E ratio

While the stock price of an organization mirrors the esteem that financial specialists are as of now setting on that investment, a stock's P/E proportion shows how much speculators will pay for each dollar of profit. The market price of a given stock is expected to ascertain its P/E proportion, however from numerous points of view, the

P/E proportion offers better understanding into the stock's development potential.

As a rule, a high P/E proportion shows that speculators expect higher income. Nonetheless, a stock with a high P/E proportion isn't really a superior investment than one with a lower P/E proportion, as a high P/E proportion can show that the stock is being exaggerated. In the event that you put resources into an exaggerated stock, you risk losing cash on the off chance that it doesn't live up to financial specialists' high-profit desires.

On the other side, when an organization's stock has a low P/E proportion, it might demonstrate that the stock is underestimated. Financial specialists can frequently purchase the underestimated stock at a rebate and afterward benefit when the price of that stock trips. All things considered, some of the time a low P/E proportion mirrors an authentic absence of development potential.

You can think about an organization's P/E proportion with that of comparable organizations in its industry to get a feeling of whether the stock you're hoping to buy is exaggerated or underestimated.

What Is the Relationship Between P/E Ratio and Stock Price?

These two unique proportions of a stock's esteem can cooperate to paint a reasonable picture.

The objective of any shrewd financial specialist ought to be to get the most ideal arrangement when acquiring stock. The better the arrangement, the higher the potential for benefit. In such manner, both an organization's P/E proportion and stock price can offer extraordinary knowledge into whether the time is more right than wrong to purchase a given stock.

CHAPTER 5

Risk Management

"Some risks that are thought to be unknown are not unknown. With some foresight and critical thought, some risks that at first glance may seem unforeseen, can, in fact, be foreseen. Armed with the right set of tools, procedures, knowledge, and insight, light can be shed on variables that lead to risk, allowing us to manage them."

—

Daniel Wagner

This Book on stock trading would be incomplete without preparing your mind about the dynamic environment you are in or about to enter. Risk management must be understood by the investor. The topic of risk management, or position sizing as it's sometimes known, is paramount to your longevity as a trader.

The bottom line really is this - the more you gamble on a single trade, the more volatile your returns will become. The more volatile your account balance is, the greater the emotional roller-coaster you will ride.

Experiencing too many ups and downs, especially large ups and downs, is not really appropriate for a career trader. It will create an unsettling environment in both your professional and personal life, and it may also adversely affect your health. It is therefore paramount to manage your risk exposure and so create some trading and health longevity for yourself.

An easy way to manage risk is to split your trading capital into equal parts. This is a very good way for starters in stock trading. But as your trading continues, you would need to develop a better risk management technique

Imagine you are a professional golfer and compete on the pro tour. The tour events are made up of four days of golf, and on each of those days, you play 18 holes. In total, you will play 72 holes. As much as you'd like to make every hole, you know that is impossible. Therefore, while you simply attempt to play as best you can, the goal that is really in the back of your mind is not to have an extremely bad hole that destroys the entire round or tournament.

In other words, you are managing your score by not doing anything that will ruin the tournament, this is also likened to an investor who is making planned single trade per time and not taking any risky shots that could lead to penalization once played against the rules. You attempt to avoid bunkers, play away from water hazards and out-of-bounds areas, and do your best to control the ball and keep it on the fairway at all times. You realize that if you fail to keep the ball on the fairway, you will be penalized harshly for the oversight.

When playing the tournaments, you are also aware of external factors that may play a part in your decisions. Factors such as the wind, recent rain or dryness, the angle of the fairways, the speed of the greens and even the competition can have an adverse impact on your game. There are also external factors such as sports critics who may influence your line of thinking.

When faced with all these factors good golfers will simply take one shot at a time. They micro-manage their game by not thinking about the absolute end result. They simply play the shot they have in front of them. They play for safety and to stay in the game for the long haul. They play each shot so as to be in some type of contention at the end of the tournament, as you can't win if you're not in contention.

If we apply this analogy to trading, hitting a bad shot into a water hazard and being penalized is like taking a much larger loss than average. We know that its not every trade that will win, just like a pro golfer will know that not every shot will be perfect. But we trade to stay in play and by that I mean we only allow a small amount of risk on each trade. When we do have some bad trades, and they are bound to occur, they will not disrupt the end game, which is to have enough capital to keep on trading.

So think like a pro golfer and divide your capital into 72 equal parts – as if each trade you make is similar to each hole a pro golfer plays in a four-day tournament. A single hole cannot be responsible for winning the tournament, but a very bad hole can certainly make it impossible to win. Good traders understand that some trades will be losers, some trades will be winners and some will be great wins, but they do their best to ensure that a single trade or even a string of losing trades will not destroy their account balances.

The probable length of a losing streak

As long as you have divided your capital into 72 equal parts and placed a protective stop, a single trade on its own is rarely destructive. However, when a string of losing trades occurs, it can be a cause for concern – both financially and emotionally. You might think that if you win up to half the time you play, a winning trade would surely follow each losing trade.

Nothing could be further from the truth. I remember waiting for a plane in Japan several years ago and being bored. I started tossing a coin to determine how often heads or tails appeared - after all, a coin only has two sides and so there is a fifty-fifty chance of a head or a tail coming up. Mathematically, I knew the outcome, but I wanted to see it for myself. Sure enough, on quite a few occasions I was able to toss a run of nine heads or tails. Runs of five were extremely common.

If you were able to mathematically ascertain the probable length of a losing streak you could better prepare yourself for its potential impact financially and emotionally - when it does occur.

Capital allocation

There is a well-known trading course sold globally that has been around for 20 or more years. The operators of this course suggest you should risk 10 percent of your initial account equity on each trade. Is this wise? I say no. What happens if the first five trades are losses? They, obviously, will tell you that it won't happen, but what if you've just paid $1000 for this great trading course and you lose 50 percent of your capital in just five trades? You'd be devastated. I say I am no better than random, or a 50 percent win rate. Therefore, according to our spreadsheet calculations, there is a possibility I could have 13 losses in a row. In light of this, I cannot bet 10 percent of my account on each trade because there is a chance I will lose more than what is in my account. Even if I bet 5 percent on each trade, after 13 losing trades my account balance would have declined by 65 percent. Is that acceptable to you? It's not to me.

There are not too many traders in the world that can do that. If we use our golfing analogy and divide our capital into 72 equal parts, we're risking just 1.39 percent of our equity on each trade. (Remember – the amount risked is the amount lost if you are stopped out of a trade, not the total amount invested.) This means that 13 consecutive losers would cause a total loss of just 18 percent. Is that acceptable to you? It certainly is to me. After making this basic calculation, we can adjust our risk on each trade to suit our own risk profile. Each person has a different risk appetite. Some people are more than happy to lose 50 percent of their account balance.

Others are comfortable with losing 20 percent of their equity. Some of you may think that such a losing streak will not happen to you. Maybe not, but do you want to put yourself in that position? I'd like to be a fly on the wall as you explain to your spouse why you've lost 65 percent of your capital in the first few weeks of your new trading career. Your friends and family will call you a gambler – and, unfortunately, if you bet too much on a single trade, that's exactly what you are.

Advanced asset allocation

This basic concept of splitting your capital into equal parts is adequate for a beginner or intermediate trader. If you wish to take the next step or you are quite conservative, the best method I have used is fixed fractional position sizing.

Fixed fractional (FF) also uses the concept of percentage risk per position but is calculated from the account balance on an on-going basis rather than the initial trading account balance. It is also very useful because it naturally compounds your account when you're profitable, yet defends it when you are having a losing streak. When using this method, a percentage risk of your account is chosen for each trade. As shown above, the higher the risk, the more you'll lose (or win) and the more volatile your account will become.

Clearly, there are two sides to the risk equation but the following three factors must be considered:

1 If you lose all your capital you will not be able to trade.

2 The more you lose, the harder it becomes mentally to continue to trade.

3 The only thing you can control is how much you lose.

Nevertheless, the risk in the stock market is very dynamic. It happens within a twinkle of an eye. If you want your money to grow up faster, you will be exposed to more risk. Risk is all over our lives. I will say "not taking a risk is a greater risk itself"

Understand the stock environment and get to know more about it, but never get scared of taking risk. What you should be concerned about are detail risk assessment and risk management, it should be your watchword as an investor. Before your investment, make your decision carefully, so your risk might get lower. There are lots of risks in the stock market.

But, what you can do is to be careful about each movement of your investment, and lower down the risk you will get. Never think that you are the luckiest person, and you will encounter no risk.

Chapter 6

Get Over Your Emotional Attachment to Money

"Look within. Be still. Free from fear and attachment, know the sweet joy of living in the way."

-Buddha

An adjustment in our financial circumstance begins with an adjustment in our point of view towards cash. Getting out the negative contemplations about cash will evacuate the blockages that are keeping cash from streaming to us.

Months back while working at a shop that sold costly gold wristwatch, I swiped the bank card of a client making a buy and it restored a mistake message. His lightning brisk reaction was, "However there is cash. I have a million in that financial balance."

There is the quick response that comes into the brain of the client. This is a humiliation!! Intuitively he reacts that he had this measure of cash in the record. That feeling or feeling of dread, tension, and disgrace emerges in the brain of the retailer.

Financial master, Suze Orman states that dread, disgrace, and outrage are the most widely recognized feelings encompassing cash.

We as a whole contemplate our bank balance. Indeed, obviously, it is that as well, however cash is additionally emphatically associated with feelings. Furthermore, before you feel that you are absolved from an enthusiastic connection to cash, reconsider.

How would you feel when you understand you are down to your last cent? Dread, frenzy, discouragement and even outrage make a mockery of, your face nearly changes.

Once in a while our emotions towards cash are strong to the point that we begin to abhor cash since we trust that it is the reason for the majority of our issues. Detest is a forceful feeling.

Cash has even been the reason a few people have endeavored suicide.

On the other side, disclose to me how you will feel on the off chance that you abruptly got news that you won the lottery, or acquired a huge aggregate of cash? Glad, isn't that so? Alleviation — end of my cash issues. I'm free! Or on the other hand so you think.

What drives our beliefs about money?

Obviously cash brings out forceful feelings and everybody has profoundly held and frequently intuitive convictions about cash. Yet, where do our sentiments about cash originate from?

Our considerations about cash frequently originate from adolescence. How our folks dealt with cash gives the establishment to how we may deal with cash. This is reason generational neediness and generational riches exists. Destitute individuals impart awful cash propensities and convictions to their youngsters. Then again, rich individuals have a tendency to impart their theories and systems on riches creation to the kids. Combined with that is the failure of destitute individuals to support encourage training for their youngsters and the preferred standpoint kids from rich homes have ideal from the begin, thus the cycle proceeds.

Add to that the way that formal tutoring does exclude financial training, thus we go forward into the world with almost no financial guide and soon we are settling on awful financial choices, running up obligation and have ourselves entrapped in a financial chaos in beside no time.

Financial analysts Bradley Klontz and Ted Klontz allude to the expression "cash content" to portray our center convictions about cash. They say that "cash contents are ordinarily oblivious, created in youth, go down from age to age inside families and societies, logically bound, and regularly just partial realities".

To discover which cash content you have going through your mind, perused the article What did your folks REALLY show you cash?

The Truth about Money

In all actuality the issue isn't cash. The issue is the manner by which we approach cash, how we consider cash and how we handle cash. Individuals who continually ponder cash, have a tendency to be tormented by cash issues as long as they can remember. Individuals who trust that cash is something inside their control, are the ones who turn out to be more effective and at last increment their cash. Those are the general population who as opposed to grumbling about their absence of cash, instruct themselves about cash. Financial insight is the reason for riches expansion.

An adjustment in our financial circumstance begins with an adjustment by the way we consider cash. Getting out the negative musings about cash will expel the blockages that are keeping cash from streaming to us.

The Disastrous Pursuit of Money

While we ought to analyze our sentiments towards cash and endeavor to oversee cash better, we ought not enable it to expend us.

We as a whole need cash to live and cash makes life simpler and more agreeable and gives us access to better administrations.

Tragically, in this day and age, cash is the focal point of numerous individuals' lives, to the weakness of their wellbeing, family, and personal satisfaction. Realism and consumerism are driving individuals. Everybody is attempting to stay aware of every other person with the best contraptions, autos, and houses. So profound is the need to awe that we feel humiliated to tell our companions we can't go along with them at that costly eatery when we don't have cash.

Once more, what is driving this? It's our feelings. We rest easy thinking about ourselves when we have the most recent iPhone or stroll around in planner marks. We need to awe individuals with how much cash we have. Cash approves us. Cash makes us feel we are someone.

On the off chance that this is your relationship to cash, you are on a dangerous slant. These are the wrong purposes behind pursuing cash. Cash should upgrade our lives, not run it.

There's nothing amiss with these things essentially. They're pleasant to have. In any case, if your reality spins around this, at that point you've lost reason. What many neglect to acknowledge is that there are more regrettable things in life than not having cash. Having no friends and family, having weakness, having no companions to offer help amid extreme occasions, having no otherworldly association, having no reason throughout everyday life.

Changing Our Attitudes Towards Money

What we ought to take a stab at is to build up a more advantageous association with cash.

Cash has such a ground-breaking sway on individuals that a sudden gain or misfortune in cash can profoundly affect a few people's identities and states of mind. It can turn a pleasant individual awful or a glad individual hopeless. It can move eagerness and narrow-mindedness. More cash can really be a terrible thing for a few people.

Be that as it may, by and large, cash won't on a very basic level change your identity or what you accept. At your center, you will in any case be a similar individual with or without cash. So also, on the off chance that you are terrible at taking care of a minimal expenditure, you'll be awful at dealing with a considerable measure of cash.

That underlying happiness at the sudden bounty of cash rapidly blurs and you go ideal back to being the manner in which you generally were. That is the reason the idiom "cash can't get you satisfaction" was begat. That underlying satisfaction is passing. There are numerous miserable rich individuals.

-The key is to find peace and contentment with or without lots of money. For once we have our focus in life clear and stop allowing money to have so much power over us, any changes in our financial

situation will have a less devastating impact on our emotions.

Financial guru Suze Orman wholes it up best. "Individuals truly haven't the faintest idea by any stretch of the imagination," she says with profound conviction. "They think the reason they are hopeless — that they are a passionate wreck — is on the grounds that they have definitely no cash. They sincerely believe that in the event that they had more cash they would have less issues. The issue is that it's not valid! The reason they don't have more cash is a result of how they feel about their life and their identity. Your identity figures out what you have and get the chance to keep. You characterize your cash. You characterize the things around you. In any case, cash and the things around you can never honestly characterize your identity.

Understand That Money Is The Reason For Investing In Stock

Investor behavior has been all around reported; there are various speculations that endeavor to explain the regret and overreaction that buyers and sellers experience when it comes to the stock market and the potential gains and losses on that money. Investors' psyche overpowers rational thinking amid times of pressure, regardless of whether that pressure is a result of euphoria or fear.

The average non-proficient financial specialist is putting his well deserved money in question and, while planning to make benefit, needs to secure that money against misfortunes. Speculators get investment "data" from numerous sources, for example, prevailing press, financial news, companions, family and colleagues. Intermittently financial specialists get tempted by the market amid times of market quiet (low instability) and delayed positively trending markets.

Buyer markets are periods when the market has a tendency to go up unpredictably. Amid such seasons of market extravagance, financial specialists have a tendency to tune in to stories from companions or relatives about how much cash they are making in the market, drumming up some excitement and convincing those not contributed to try things out.

Similarly, when financial specialists read tales about a terrible economy or hear reports about an unstable or negative market period, fear assumes control and they offer at the base. (Not all speculators are rationally arranged for when a much-anticipated positively trending market at long last comes charging in.

Wrong Timing

The slack between when an occasion happens and when it is accounted for is the thing that regularly makes speculators lose cash. The media will report a positively trending market just once it has just hit; except if the pattern proceeds with, stocks will withdraw in up and coming periods.

Speculators, impacted by the reports, frequently pick these seasons of premium valuations to develop their portfolios. It is troubling when the day by day stock market report begins the standard news since it makes a buzz and speculators settle on choices dependent on "assessments" that are regularly obsolete. Market vulnerability makes fear and achieves a climate of passionate investing.

Search For the Bright Spot

In spite of the solid propensities that speculators depict at the pinnacles and valleys, they have become different periods remedy. All through the 1990s, there was a consistent stream of assets into the market amid a period when the market was on a delayed bull run.

In like manner from 2004 to 2007 amid another solid positively trending market, financial specialists emptied cash into the market. So it tends to be conjectured that amid times of next to no unpredictability, (for example, delayed buyer markets), speculators turn out to be more agreeable in the market and start to contribute.

Nonetheless, amid times of instability, or when bull or bear markets start and end consistently, cash streams have a tendency to reflect disarray and the planning of the streams end up jumbled with real market development. (Find how some odd human inclinations can happen in the market. Is it true that we are extremely balanced?

Tested Strategies to Eliminate Emotions Out of Investing

Speculator returns failed to meet expectations in connection to the genuine finances' profits more than ten years, as indicated by Morning Star. For instance, there was a 2.49% hole in returns between the normal financial specialist and reserve toward the finish of 2013. The proof recommends that enthusiastic investing defeats the run of the mill financial specialist amid times of vulnerability. There are techniques, be that as it may, that can mitigate the mystery and diminish the impact of inadequately timing asset streams.

The best has a tendency to be the dollar-cost averaging of investment dollars. Dollar-cost averaging is where square with measures of dollars are contributed at a general, foreordained interim. This methodology is great amid all market conditions.

Amid a descending pattern, financial specialists are acquiring shares at less expensive and less expensive prices. Amid an upward pattern, the offers already held in the portfolio are delivering capital additions and less offers are being included at the higher price. The way to this system is to keep with it set the procedure and don't mess with it except if a noteworthy change warrants returning to and rebalancing the built up course. (There is in excess of one approach to work this procedure.

Another system to decrease the passionate reaction to market investing is to expand a portfolio. There have been just a bunch of times in history when all markets have moved as one and broadening gave little security. In most typical market cycles, utilizing an expansion methodology gives descending assurance.

Enhancing a portfolio can take numerous structures - investing in various enterprises, diverse topographies, and distinctive kinds of investments and notwithstanding supporting with elective investments like land and private value. There are unmistakable market conditions that support each of these subsectors of the market, so a portfolio made up of all these different kinds of investments ought to give assurance in a scope of market conditions.

The Truth

Investing without feeling is simpler said than done, particularly on the grounds that vulnerability manages the market and the media. Proof proposes that most financial specialists are enthusiastic and amplify cash streams at the wrong occasions - a surefire approach to lessen potential returns.

Systems that take out the enthusiastic reaction to investing should create restores that are essentially more noteworthy than those shown by the commonplace financial specialist reacting to the market as opposed to proactively investing in the market. Dollar-cost averaging and broadening are two demonstrated systems inside a large number of different choices to decrease a speculator's enthusiastic response to the market.

Highlights:

1. To succeed in stocks, you must keep your feet on the ground. In other words, clearly make sure you follow the trends and keep track of latest reports, if possible secure the services of a financial advisor and a good stockbroker.

2. Remember the popular Chicken Little story, when they say the sky is falling pause and let your logic rule over human emotions.

3. Whenever others are forced to consider pulling out of a market in its heights or its lows search for the bright spot.

4. Listen to Reports, news on latest trends on stocks but keep this in mind if all the

reports were true, there would be no losers in the stock market.

5. Money is not real, it is a piece of note we all chose to give value to, if you wish to win in the stock market focus on more real things like data, statistics and industries you understand and always trade on data and not emotions.

Chapter 7

Invest In Something You Know a Lot and Care About

"Know what you own, and know why you own it."

- Peter Lynch

Do your homework before making a decision. And once you've made a decision, make sure to re-evaluate your portfolio on a timely basis. A wise holding today may not be a wise holding in the future.

Most people have a stock market strategy I personally call google news strategy. They wake up in the morning and listen to the news or read a blog and hear that a stock is on the rise in an industry they clearly know nothing or care about and they jump into it and boom!! they own stocks, with no idea of its growth or how the company functions.

Having an idea of an industry doesn't just give you a little edge it gives you a 70% over 30% advantage, to succeed and in specifics, it's far easier to analyze a stock you quite know a lot about and understand.

Data can also easily be source since there is a direct understanding of the system or industry.

Invest In What You Know

As speculators, we trust it is conceivable to gauge a scope of inherent incentive for an organization dependent on its financial explanations and filings. This is impossible, be that as it may, in the event that you don't see how an organization profits. In the event that, for instance, you don't know anything about adverts and printing industry, you shouldn't put resources into Noella Technologies. Why? Except if you comprehend the organization's items, market, aggressive qualities and shortcomings, you won't have the capacity to extend the future money streams.

In his productions, works and addresses, well known speculator Warren Buffett regularly talks about the idea of a "hover of skill". This hover of capability comprises of the considerable number of organizations with which the financial specialist is well-known and altogether gets it. A speculator that has put over the most recent ten years as a checker at a supermarket would have leeway while examining the financial explanations of a market chain; he or she would have the capacity to pinpoint qualities and shortcomings of the business, assess the aggressive atmosphere of the business, and analyze the execution of an imminent investment against those of an amazing food merchant.

The span of a speculator's hover of fitness isn't as essential as obviously characterizing the fringes. In the event that you are new to the protection business, don't endeavor to assess the execution of a property and loss organization. Moreover, on the off chance that you don't comprehend the Internet, don't tried requesting the yearly report of an Internet stock. Straying from the hover of capability drives a future financial specialist into the place where there is theory.

Finding High yielding Investment Stock

How would you discover organizations you can get it? Travel to your nearby shopping center and investigate the stores to perceive what is well known. Focus on where your children need you to take them for school year kickoff shopping.

Dwindle Lynch, a standout amongst the best cash administrators ever, got a portion of his best investing thoughts from tuning in to his significant other and kids after they returned from running errands. Truth be told, Lynch purchased stock in Hanes after his better half brought home the recently presented L'eggs she found while in the checkout line at the supermarket; the investment made millions.

Another approach to get investment thoughts is to experience your wash room, organizers, pantry, and carport to discover items you utilize frequently. Most names contain data on the item's maker.

As you should comprehend that any organization prepared to meet a particular need that is inadequate in your territory and has the correct administration is certain to be a HIT, and such stocks could cost as low as couple of dollars per share yet could ascend to a thousand times their unique totals following couple of months or years.

Price Still Matters

Discovering organizations that are straightforward is just the start. The hover of fitness test ought to just be a beginning stage to create a rundown of investment conceivable outcomes dependent on a financial specialist's qualities and bits of knowledge.

An organization should in any case show amazing financial aspects, an appealing price, and investor amicable administration. Whenever found, these sacred vessel investments are certain to deliver stellar returns for the speculator's wallet.

Invest In What You Care About

Investing in what you care about is the best definition of passion on display, the advantages are so enormous that if you could pick only one thing from this book, it is this key.

I learned many years ago in my quest to master stock trading and investing that the wisest choice and most yielding idea is investing in what you care and know a lot about.

The reason for this is simple because when the market goes down and it will at some point. You can ride the storm out and know why you purchased the stock. Allowing you not to invest on emotion like the Sheep mentality do.

Greater Fool Theory

In the stock market, this is the point at which an extraordinary number of speculators make a faulty investment, with the presumption that they will have the capacity to offer it later to "a greater fool". At the end of the day, they purchase something not on account of the trust that it merits the price, but instead in light of the fact that they trust that they will have the capacity to pitch it to another person at a significantly higher price. It is additionally called survivor investing. It is comparative in idea to the Keynesian beauty contest guideline of stock investing.

The greater fool theory expresses that you can benefit from investing insofar as there is a greater fool than yourself to purchase the investment at a higher price. This implies you could profit from an overpriced stock as long as another person will pay more to get it from you.

In the long run, you come up short on fools as the market for any investment overheats. Investing as indicated by the greater fool theory implies overlooking valuations, income reports and the various information. Disregarding information is as dangerous as giving careful consideration to it, thus individuals attributing to the greater fool theory could be left holding the short end of the stick after a market rectification.

How to Avoid Being a "Greater Fool"

Since you have comprehended this idea, it's more imperative to abstain from being the greater fool than just to know the theory.

Anyway, it's very easy to abstain from being a greater fool. Furthermore, here's the manner by which you can do it-"Before influencing your investment in any advantages, to do your very own investigation and research. Don't aimlessly pursue the group, paying ever more elevated price with no reason."

Numerous individuals put resources into a few stocks since it's stock price is going higher and expanding too quick. In spite of the fact that they realize that the price of that stock can't be steady at that expanded price, still they will enter the stock with the desire to exit soon enough making a few benefits.

On the off chance that you need to abstain from being a greater fool, abstain from acquiring a stock since its price is expanding. Control your eagerness to profit by nonsensically purchasing over-priced stocks just with an instinct that you can auction it later at even a higher price.

We should attempt to separate how to abstain from being a "greater fool"

• Do not indiscriminately pursue the group, paying increasingly elevated prices for something with no valid justification

• Do your examination and pursue an arrangement

- Adopt a long haul technique for investments to maintain a strategic distance from air pockets

- Diversify your portfolio

- Control your ravenousness and oppose the impulse to attempt to profit inside a brief timeframe

- Understand that there is no certain thing in the market, not by any means persistent price swelling

The most critical and surest method for getting away from the greater fool theory is for you to put resources into what you care about and something your will to pay your time and assets to truly get it.

Chapter 8

10 Quick to do's for any Investor

Here are 10 Quick to-do lists and a summary of the details in the previous chapters

1. Avoid the herd mentality

2. Take informed decision

3. Invest in business you understand

4. Don't try to time the market

5. Follow a disciplined investment approach

6. Do not let emotions cloud your judgment

7. Create a broad portfolio

8. Have realistic expectations

9. Invest only your surplus funds

10. Monitor rigorously

NEW BOOK: CONSISTENT WEALTH GENERATION AND ITS MAINTENANCE

PROLOGUE

Making money from stocks is actually easy and cool right? However, this is just a step to generate wealth.

It is one advantage to get exposed to the strategies to make money, it is an additional advantage to discover more strategies to continual generation and maintenance of wealth.

This second series would be enlightening us on how to continually generate wealth with the consciousness of the risks available and how to maintain these wealth. In this wise, we would be supporting the saying that goes thus: "the reward of hard work is hard work" This in context literarily implies that the reward of more cash is more cash.

A lot of individuals especially investors fresh on the field get overwhelmed after acquiring cool cash from the stock market. In the end, they get carried away and finally lavish the whole cash. This book would lead investors, both new and professionals on the field on how to make more money and how to maintain the cash to yield more profitable results.

About the book

Investment!!!Trading!!!Stock Trading!!! A couple of investors wants to hit the million or billion dollar mark from stock trading but they fail to understand that making money from stock trading is a master plan.

"How to make money in stocks" is a book you must read. It is comprehensive, simple, and insightful and designed for you to profit from trading in stock. You can journey from penury to plenty as you read.